chocolate chips
and
CHARITY

VISITING TEACHING
— in the —
REAL WORLD

COMPILED BY
LINDA HOFFMAN
KIMBALL

PRAISE FOR *CHOCOLATE CHIPS AND CHARITY*

"Two reasons I already love *Chocolate Chips and Charity: Visiting Teaching in the Real World*—first, it includes some of my favorite writers, and second, it has chocolate in the title. What could be bad?"

—Louise Plummer

"I think Linda and her friends wrote this book for me. I recently attended the funeral of a woman I was assigned to visit teach years ago, who had confided to me way back then that she was ready to come back to the Church. One step at a time, she did come back, and two months before her death, she was endowed.

"As I saw her in her casket, in temple clothes, I was moved by the thought that I had played a small part in opening the door for her. Yet I am busy, and visiting teaching often feels like a burden. What a wonderful thing for someone so full of good will and generosity and humor as Linda Hoffman Kimball to put this book together for me and then offer it to every other visiting teacher or teachee who needs to remember how light and joyful—and sometimes miraculous—the burden really is."

—Margaret Blair Young

"Linda Hoffman Kimball observes that 'Visiting Teachers change light bulbs, diapers, and lives.' What she doesn't tell you is that this small gem of a book may change the way you view Visiting Teaching itself. I loved *Chocolate Chips and Charity.*"

—Ann Edwards Cannon

chocolate chips
and
CHARITY

VISITING TEACHING
in the
REAL WORLD

Linda Hoffman Kimball

CFI
AN IMPRINT OF CEDAR FORT, INC.
SPRINGVILLE, UTAH

ISBN 13: 978-1-4621-1110-7

Published by CFI, an imprint of Cedar Fort, Inc.
2373 W. 700 S., Springville, UT 84663
Distributed by Cedar Fort, Inc., www.cedarfort.com

LIBRARY OF CONGRESS CATALOGING-IN-PUBLICATION DATA

Kimball, Linda Hoffman, author.
  Chocolate chips and charity / Linda Hoffman Kimball.
    pages cm
  ISBN 978-1-4621-1110-7 (alk. paper)
  1. Church work with women--Church of Jesus Christ of Latter-day Saints. 2. Visitations (Church work) 3. Relief Society (Church of Jesus Christ of Latter-day Saints) 4. Mormon women--Religious life. I. Title.

  BX8643.W4K56 2012
  264'.449332--dc23

                    2012015487

Cover design by Rebecca J. Greenwood
Cover design © 2012 by Lyle Mortimer
Edited and typeset by Emily S. Chambers

Printed in the United States of America

10 9 8 7 6 5 4 3 2 1

Printed on acid-free paper

❧ **For my sisters** ❧

2 May 2015

My dear sweet Ellen,

I am so proud of you and the woman you have become - a woman of faith and action. As you have shared your desires for the women you will be serving as Relief Society President, I have been overwhelmed with gratitude for your strong desire to serve the Lord and His daughters.

Visiting Teaching is such a profound part of how we serve each other as sisters that I thought this book might be an inspiration to you. I'm sorry I have not been a better example to you in this area.

I know that as you seek the Lord's guidance that you will be able to magnify your calling and encourage the Lord's love to be increased among the sisters in your ward. The covenants you have made - both at baptism and in the temple - will give you great spiritual power and insight.

I love you.

Mom

Mosiah 18:21
D&C 12:8

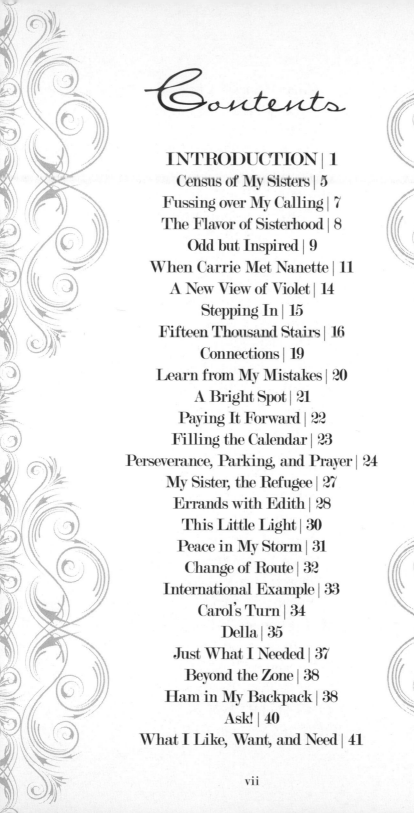

Contents

Contents

Introduction

Visiting Teachers Change Light Bulbs, Diapers, and Lives

VISITING TEACHING HAS been part of Latter-day Saint practice since the earliest days of the Church. As early as 1843, Emma Smith, first president of the Relief Society, recommended the formation of a committee whose objective was to "search out the poor and suffering, to call upon the rich for aid, and thus as far as possible, relieve the wants of all" (*Encyclopedia of Mormonism*, p. 1517).

In our day the purpose remains the same. Simply put, visiting teaching helps us learn to take care of each other. By extending beyond ourselves to meet the needs of others, we follow Jesus' divine example. Visiting teaching is the Lord's way of helping us mortal, temporal beings become like Jesus Christ. It provides structure for our core Christian impulse to emulate our Master's life of selfless service. Through this process we harvest other delights—sisterhood, connection, love, care, support, friendship. But at the heart of visiting teaching is always the willingness to take care of each other as Jesus would.

Many times a kind expression—a few words of counsel, or even a warm or affectionate shake of the hand—will do more good and be better appreciated than a purse of gold."
—Eliza R. Snow

President Spencer W. Kimball expressed vividly the Christlike mission of visiting teaching: "'Watch over the Church always'—not twenty minutes a month but always— 'and be with and strengthen them'—not a knock at the door, but to be with them and lift them, and strengthen them and empower them, and fortify them" (*Encyclopedia of Mormonism*, p. 1517).

Visiting teachers take care of each other in myriad ways. Typically, visiting teachers share supportive gospel-centered messages and pray for and with the sisters they visit. They take note of the sisters' spiritual and temporal needs. They provide service in crisis and support through the humdrum. They give casseroles, rides to the airport, and shoulders to cry on. They change light bulbs, diapers, and lives.

Visiting teaching is a reciprocal arrangement. Sisters who are visiting teachers are also visit taught. Caring for each other flows in all directions. Strangers' lives intersect. Familiar friends see each other in new lights. In the circular way so familiar to a system where God's ways are "one eternal round," sisters learn by teaching and teach by learning.

The Spirit is the best guide for visiting teachers seeking to know how best to meet the needs of the sisters in their care. Eliza R. Snow, another nineteenth-century Relief Society president, acknowledged some of the subtle merits of visiting teaching: "Many times a kind expression—a few words of counsel, or even a warm or affectionate shake of the hand—will do more good and be better appreciated than a purse of gold" (General Board, 1966, p. 40).

We live in a world that seems increasingly fragile and precarious. We long for reassurance and safety, consolation and support. Besides the traumas of physical, spiritual, and political unrest around the globe, we face unique challenges on every front. There are bounties and cautions with the enormous technological advances of our era. Our children face opportunities and opposition hardly imaginable generations ago. Health and financial pressures continue but in new configurations. Balancing the intricacies of family, career, education, and hectic schedules requires a circus performer's skill.

There is vast potential for our lives to be fragmented and isolated—even in a whirling cloud of activity. We need all the reminders we can get that "it is upon the rock of our Redeemer, who is Christ, the Son of God, that [we] must build our foundation . . . a foundation whereon if [we] build [we] cannot fall" (Helaman 5:12).

Part of the challenge is to keep visiting teaching from becoming one more obligation and one more pressure. How do we do that?

One way is to keep our focus on the purpose of visiting teaching. Through this system of taking care of one another, the Relief Society creed resonates: "We are beloved spirit daughters of God, and our lives have meaning, purpose, and direction. As a worldwide sisterhood, we are united in our devotion to Jesus Christ, our Savior and Exemplar." This is a perfect pairing with the long-standing motto of Relief Society: "Charity Never Faileth."

Another way is to share insight and inspiration with each other. When we see how flexibility, faith, courage, creativity, consistency, and good humor help others, we are bolstered as well.

In this volume, visiting teachers of many ages and backgrounds express with candor and compassion their experiences with the strengths, realities, and occasional pitfalls of the program. Some of our listed contributors are descendants of pioneers, others are converts, others are somewhere in between. Some are or have been Relief Society presidents or visiting teaching supervisors. Others are brand new to visiting teaching. We won't tell you who is who. Sit back, get comfortable and enjoy. This is a conversation. We hope it will stimulate thoughts and conversations for you as well.

With the exception of Emma Lou Thayne's poem, references to blog posts, print sources, and occasional quotes from Relief Society leaders past and present, no attribution is given to our listed contributors in an effort to preserve everyone's privacy. Some details have been changed toward the same end.

The goal is insight, not guilt— enthusiasm, not dread.

These offerings are varied. There are short suggestions, pithy bits of wisdom, personal vignettes, and longer accounts from authentic experiences. Some are funny, some touching, some thought-provoking. From the poignant to the practical, each is honest and shared toward a common goal. That goal is insight, not guilt—enthusiasm, not dread. The hope is that this collection will renew your affection and commitment to visiting teaching. Perhaps this month you can make your appointments or open your own door knowing that when guided by the Holy Ghost, surprising, wonderful and even holy things can happen.

—Linda Hoffman Kimball
Evanston, Illinois & Woodland, Utah
May 2012

CENSUS OF MY SISTERS

I READ AN ARTICLE that talked about the potential ramifications of the "I'm a Mormon" series of commercials and suggested that perhaps one result of the commercials is that members of the Church will see the Church differently—as a more diverse and inclusive community. I wondered. I went to Mormon.org and watched twenty or thirty of the videos. I felt my inner cynic creeping up on me. Is this really a representation of the Church? All those people were *so* cool. And they so carefully represented all the colors of the human rainbow. Is this really who we are? Or is it just a TV version of our cool diversity?

I decided to do a very simple census. I made a list of every sister that I have had on my visiting teaching list for the last ten years. Here they are:

- A college lacrosse star.

- A mother of three, who borrowed my vacuum, pawned it, and used the money for drugs.

- A Nigerian medical student.

- A state senator's wife.

- Two Filipina women. One old and one young. Both homesick for their country. I served them by eating all the food they cooked for me.

- A Haitian woman who worked 80+ hours a week to not only help support her husband and children but to also supply all of the school fees and supplies for her extended family back in Haiti.

- One Venezuelan stay-at-home mom who always

tried to sell us stuff she'd bought down the street at
Walmart—for a substantial profit. I still have a backpack I bought from her.

- A Jamaican paralegal.
- An elderly animal lover. When she was in the hospital, I cleaned her cats' litter boxes. And committed to
  never getting a cat.
- A Texan escaping an abusive marriage.
- A woman currently in an abusive marriage.
- A Colombian single mother. We took her out to lunch
  one day at the worst Chinese restaurant I've ever been
  too. She had good advice: "Order the shrimp and broc-
  coli. It's impossible to make cat look like shrimp."
- A native New Yorker—born on the steps of the hospital because her mother refused to leave the musical she
  was attending before it was over.
- A Californian who decided to become an Iowa farmer
  in her late thirties.
- An uber-organized branch librarian who was seriously
  thrilled to learn she'd been secretly nick-named the "library Nazi" by branch members.
- A half-Japanese, half-Jewish heiress to a bio-engineer-
  ing company, who once spent an entire day stringing
  leis for my daughters.

Eight are single and nine are married. Some are students,
some work, some are stay-at-home moms and some are retired.
Their average number of children is 2.29. Most chose to join
the Church as adults, and just one is descended from pioneers.
They range in age from eighteen to eighty-two.

These seventeen women do not just represent the Church
for me. They *are* the Church for me.

I think that visiting teaching is most like what Christ would do if He came to earth. I think He'd come to your home, see if He could help, give you a spiritual thought, and watch over you.

FUSSING OVER MY CALLING

SOME YEARS AGO I was in a Primary presidency when our stake president called me to be a counselor in the stake Relief Society. I loved the Primary and felt strongly that I should stay in that calling. The stake president suggested I talk to the stake Relief Society president. I made an appointment to visit with her. The night before that visit, I prayed long and hard about what I should do. Later I tossed and turned in bed, thinking of all I would be giving up if I left Primary—seeing the Sunbeams fold their arms tightly during prayer, watching Kyle stop running in the hall every time he saw me.

The next morning when I went outside to change the water on the lawn, three girls in my ward rode by on their bikes, all calling excitedly over and over, "Hi, Sister Jones! Hi, Sister Jones!" I felt my prayers had been answered by these little girls. I needed to stay in Primary.

I went to my appointment with the stake Relief Society president ready to tell her why I couldn't accept the calling. After I explained my feelings about Primary, she said, "You know, children have a lot of people fuss over them. They have their parents, their grandparents, school teachers, Primary teachers, and lots of people. But many times women have no one to fuss over them."

The Spirit touched my heart. I knew I wanted to be a fusser of women. Young mothers definitely need fussing over. Single sisters need it. Even happily married women rarely have anyone who really fusses over them. We all need to be fussed over. I know because I like it so much when I've been fussed over. One month when I was sick, my visiting teacher brought me some cough medicine in a little bottle. Another sister sent me tickets to the Utah Valley Symphony where she was a soloist. Another brought me fresh juice that I hid in the fridge and drank only a tiny glass a day to make it last. I love how my current visiting teacher always speaks to me at church and makes me feel like I am one of her best friends. I like being fussed over, and I like being a fusser of women.

THE FLAVOR OF SISTERHOOD

SHORTLY AFTER MY third child was born, I was assigned a new set of visiting teachers. I didn't know either of them very well. One was a young graduate student. The other was a working mom with children several years older than mine. They were a great pair. They took my schedule into account. They gave thoughtful, brief messages and asked about my life and how I was doing. They were consistent and attentive and genuine.

Over the months we swapped stories and got acquainted. We talked about our common struggles—adjustments to school, marriage, parenthood—and about our common delights—good movies, great books, excellent music (though there our tastes diverged somewhat). I learned about one sister's cravings for Fruit Loops and the other's secret crush on the Channel 7 weather man. I even grew comfortable enough to admit my own peculiar ritual of making and freezing chocolate chip cookie dough and (as a kind of quantity control) cooking up just one cookie every night in my little toaster oven.

When my baby was nearing a year old, I became extremely fatigued and began having serious digestive problems. I went to the doctor who put me on a liquid diet for a week while she ran tests. I worried a lot about what might be wrong. I grew weary of juice and water and the occasionally sanctioned rice-in-broth "treat." I waited anxiously for the test results.

The test said I had an intestinal parasite. No, I hadn't been drinking from mountain streams or eating fruit in a third world country. I apparently picked it up at a pizza place in our town. Enormous pills got me back into working order fairly quickly, but I had to work my way back slowly to normal foods.

Just when I was able to eat a real meal again, my visiting teachers arrived with proof that they knew and loved me. What they brought was better than tuna casserole. Better than dinner rolls. They brought sisterhood in a freezer bag—a batch of homemade chocolate chip cookie dough ready to be chipped off nightly, one cookie at a time, and baked in my little toaster oven.

ODD BUT INSPIRED

Y EARS AGO, ONE of the women in my charge suffered a miscarriage. Although she already had six children, the loss of this much-desired seventh child greatly upset and disappointed her. She had a loving husband, six half-grown children, a mother, and sisters all hovering, so it was apparent that she did not need any physical help from me, but I still wanted to make a gesture of my concern.

I decided to go to Harmon's, the only candymakers in town, to buy some of their hand-dipped chocolates. I knew this sister made chocolates each year at Christmastime and would appreciate that they were special. When I entered Harmon's, I was confronted with a large case displaying a dozen or more different kinds of hand-dipped chocolates. My mouth watered. I looked at all the various chocolates with every intention of buying some for her. A few minutes later I came out of the store with a brown paper bag of black jelly beans.

When I got home with the candy I was embarrassed about taking them to her. The choice of jelly beans seemed so odd and they were cheap, not half as much as I had intended to spend for a gift. But because I had other commitments and no more time for shopping, I forced myself to take them to her anyway despite my embarrassment.

I knocked on her door. When she let me in we sat down and visited a while. Then I handed her the little gift. She opened the bag and began to weep. "How did you know that black jelly beans were my favorite candy?" she asked.

Since that day there has been a special bond between us. We have together recognized that this curious coincidence has no better explanation than that the Spirit used me to offer a special measure of love and comfort on a difficult occasion.

WHEN CARRIE MET NANETTE

IPUT MY FOOT in my mouth every time I visit taught Carrie. Like the third time I visited and asked her how often her daughter saw Carrie's ex-husband—after all, Carrie didn't wear a wedding ring, was listed as single in her Church records, and had talked about being lonely, living with her just daughter.

Carrie smiled, amused at my question and explained that she was married, pointing to the picture of her husband in a bamboo frame on the living room coffee table. I was too embarrassed to try and figure out what I was missing.

Carrie was a smart architect, living alone with her eight-year-old daughter in her stylishly decorated mid-century house. She had been inactive for years but was amenable to my coming over to visit teach her every couple of months. Still, I could sense a wariness each time she had me over. As I tried to ask her questions about herself, she gave the shortest possible answer. For a few months, I didn't go see her, tired of trying to force a bond that wasn't happening. But her mom came to visit from Utah and met me at church. She called me a few times, asking me to be her daughter's friend so she would go back to church. So I went back. Each time I felt dumb, like an unwelcome salesperson who was tolerated in order to hasten my departure.

One month, my companionship changed. Nanette had been baptized for three months. She proudly told people that she grew up in the ghettos of St. Louis. She didn't have a lot of formal education, but she was "street smart."

"You have to be to survive there," she explained matter-of-factly. She spoke loudly and plainly.

Nanette often gave me child-rearing advice, "Your boys need some discipline! Spare the whip and spoil the child!" she told me after observing me wrestle my one- and three-year-old boys throughout sacrament meeting one Sunday.

I had planned to skip visiting Carrie that first night Nanette and I went visiting teaching. I was always so careful, and yet the visits were awkward. What would Nanette say? I didn't know her well, but I knew she had the fire of a new convert, and I knew she would share her opinions. Would she tell Carrie her daughter was too skinny or ask her why she didn't come to church?

After our assigned visits, I rethought things. The evening had gone well. Nanette was thoroughly enjoying this new visiting teaching thing, and she had given lovely, heartfelt prayers at our other sisters' houses. I changed my mind. Maybe it would be easier to visit Carrie with Nanette by my side.

So I asked if she was up for a drop-by at Carrie's.

Carrie was surprised when she opened the door. She seemed frazzled and upset. Her house didn't look right. She let us in, and Nanette introduced herself. I could tell immediately that Nanette put Carrie at ease. The awkwardness between Carrie and I had disappeared as the two of them spoke. Nanette got Carrie to talk about things in ten minutes that I hadn't learned for two years, like how Carrie's husband was a Jew who lived in Switzerland, that she hated being an architect, and that they were saving up money so she and her daughter could move to where her husband was and she could be a stay-at-home mom.

Then Carrie asked Nanette about herself. Nanette explained that she sold fraud protection.

Carrie stopped.

"You know . . . my house was burglarized last night. They didn't take a lot of our stuff, but they found our passports, our birth certificates. All of that identification that I had been gathering for our next trip to Switzerland."

Nanette spent the rest of the evening walking Carrie through the necessary steps to ensure that these burglars wouldn't be able to steal her identity. She spent the next week checking up on her, helping her feel safe in her home, and following up with more helpful advice.

Nanette loved Carrie, and Carrie loved Nanette. Their bond was immediate, though on the surface the convert and lapsed-Mormon appeared to have nothing in common. Carrie did move to Switzerland, quietly and without letting us know, but I'd like to think that God sent Nanette to show her that God remembered Carrie and loved her.

For me, visiting teaching has sometimes been an exercise in learning to love someone I don't like and never will like. Strangely, some of the people I'm most excited to see in the next life are those people, because I so look forward to the day when they are healed from the sins of others that have injured them and are largely responsible for the behaviors that are less than likeable.

A NEW VIEW OF VIOLET

WHEN I WAS a young bride-to-be, Violet was my visiting teacher. Violet was alternately domineering and timid. She gave overlong, guilt-inducing messages and never made eye contact. She lived alone on modest means near and under the shadow of her turbulent family. There was always a distance and awkwardness in her visits.

When I was a month from my wedding, to my surprise Violet announced that she wanted to have a bridal shower for me. She asked me for a guest list, arranged refreshments potluck style and, on the appointed day, welcomed everyone into my apartment. It's true that she greeted people with a half smile, an icy handshake, and averted eyes, but there she stood, my dedicated visiting teacher.

Despite Violet's constant chill, the shower was a warm and wonderful event. My friends brought good wishes and a mountain of kitchen wares. Amazingly—as if she hadn't done enough already—Violet had a gift for me too. I knew it must have stretched her limited budget. I was overwhelmed with gratitude, affection, and awe for this woman whom I hadn't even really liked.

After the shower, Violet was still socially awkward, gave droning messages, and stayed too long at her visits. But I had come to see her in a different light. I remembered the New Testament story of the widow's mite:

Jesus sat over against the treasury, and beheld how the people cast money into the treasury; and many that were rich cast in much. *And there came a certain poor widow, and she threw in two mites, which make a farthing. And he called unto him his disciples, and saith unto them, Verily I say unto you, That this poor widow hath cast more in, than all they which have cast into the treasury: For all they did cast in of their abundance; but she of her want did cast in all that she had, even all her living (Mark 12:41–44).*

I knew I had been the recipient of Violet's "widow's mite" of service and generosity. Thirty-five years later I am still in awe.

STEPPING IN

S OMETIMES YOU SERVE your visiting teachee's *family* in spite of the visiting teachee. You show your love for her and for her family by stepping in when it's appropriate. That was the situation my companion and I faced when a mom couldn't see the need and, because of her own problems, was incapable of responding.

My visiting teaching companion and I have visit taught a less-active woman for years. Her still-active ex-husband continues to bring the children to church even though they live with her. We've loved and hoped and prayed for these kids to somehow survive their situation. The oldest child—a daughter—is a particular miracle. Somehow, with her parents splitting up when she was thirteen, instead of turning rebellious and difficult, she had the inner strength to stay kind, sweet, present, and engaged—while developing some spectacular talents as well.

Toward the end of college, she fell in love with a young

man and a Salt Lake Temple wedding ensued. The mom had a lot of say in what the faraway Salt Lake City reception would be like, but things got complicated many states away on our home turf. We decided, like many visiting teaching companionships before us, that we could help by hosting a wedding reception for the couple, and they could invite local congregation and community friends.

So many sisters pitched in! They made a party out of getting ready for the event. A whole team of sisters spent a morning around a granite kitchen island, making curried chicken salad, chopping, and chatting. The gal with professional floral experience did the flowers. I've done a couple of wedding cakes and dreamed up a multi-tiered confection in the wedding colors. One fellow in our ward is a designer, and he pulled in just in time to put all the fresh flowers on the cake. The reception was at my visiting teaching companion's lovely home. The talented couple sang a beautiful and moving duet as part of the evening. Grandparents flew in from the West. It was lovely.

And where was Mom? Though she was there for the setup, come seven thirty she disappeared and reappeared when it was over. It's complicated. Life just sometimes is.

FIFTEEN THOUSAND STAIRS

I STARED AT THE list of names the Relief Society president had just handed to me. These were the women I was supposed to visit teach. Thirteen of them.

"But," I whuffed, "how am I going to get to all of these? I work full time. I take a class one night a week. I'm typing up stuff at home for George's dissertation. I . . . I . . . I . . ."

Sister Anderson thumped me on the back. I wasn't sure whether it was an encouraging pat or a whack meant to block another string of excuses.

"Do the best you can," she said. "Most of them are inactive."

Which meant what? That my partner and I would be turned away and therefore cut down on that list of thirteen visitees? Or that we'd have to spend extra time bringing those women back to activity?

Sister Anderson sighed. "We just don't have enough active women in your part of the ward."

Our part of the ward, back in 1958, was the Queens part of the Manhattan Ward in New York City. Active members in that part of the city were few and far between.

I managed a smile. "Okay, we'll do it." I hoped my partner would agree. She didn't "go to business" as they say in New York, but she did have a small baby who would have to be the third member of our visiting teaching team.

When I showed the list to my partner, she echoed what I'd already said: "We'll do it."

And we did. It took us a whole week each month, visiting three women on each of the two weeknights I was free and finishing up with all of the working women on Saturday. It was difficult, and it seemed as if we just finished one month when the next month was upon us.

Two of our women lived in fifth-floor walk-up apartments. Two lived on the fourth floor, also a walk up. Several were third-floor dwellers. No elevator, except for freight or emergencies. Thankfully, several lived on the second floor, and two actually lived in houses.

Trudging up all of those stairs was the hardest part of the whole job. We liked the women. Two were active; the others were not. Some of these barely tolerated our visits, but others welcomed us cordially and fed us cookies.

Sister Richter was one of the latter. A fifth-floor dweller, she was a small lady with a thick German accent and a talent for making wonderful *Pfeffernüsse* and *Springerle*.

But she wasn't interested in renewing her attendance at church. She had been baptized in Germany, but since coming to the United States she hadn't felt comfortable in the meetings.

We went to her small apartment every month. We climbed more than eighty stairs to get there. We ate stacks of cookies, and we brought her "the message."

One week, we counted the stairs we climbed to visit all of our women. Approximately 465 we figured. That added up to more than 15,000 stairs per year if we faithfully did our job.

One hot summer day these projected 15,000 stairs seemed too much. My partner's baby was getting heavy and was teething. I'd had a hard week at work, and the class I was taking was demanding. George had a tall stack of research for me to type at home.

"It's too much," I said.

My partner agreed. Her life was not uncomplicated either.

That was the day of our last visit to our little German lady. Two days later, her son called to tell us she'd died of a heart attack. "She asked for a church funeral," he said. "She said she wanted those nice girls who visited her every month to speak."

At his request, we picked out the dress for her to be buried in. We arranged the funeral program with one of the fine singers of the ward doing a couple of solos in German. My partner and I spoke, as requested. And George, whom she'd met and liked, gave the sermon for her German friends in their own language.

For my partner and me, those projected 15,000 stairs we climbed to do our visiting teaching seemed like a small price to pay for bringing a soul back to church, if only in death.

CONNECTIONS

Some of my best visiting teaching experiences have been somewhat unorthodox. In our new Salt Lake City ward, husbands and wives are assigned together when possible. Our partnership and traditional approach work out well for three on our list. The other three are never seen at church and in one case requested no contact—ever. Since I was the new neighbor from the Midwest, I wrote a casual note of introduction and indicated I would be dropping by, and I did—solo. The "no contact" lady was delightful. Although she knew I came from the Church, she did not seem to mind my just showing up for a visit. Occasionally I would bring fresh corn or a cool treat on a hot day. I did not give a formal message. I believe we established meaningful contact—a good beginning.

It took almost a year to catch another sister with a very busy schedule. I had dropped off notes, small gifts, and invitations and was hanging a valentine on her door when she answered and invited me in. I discovered she was recuperating from surgery. I felt sorry I had not been of assistance, but as we discussed medical experiences and personnel, I inquired if she knew Dr. Fox. She replied that she knew of him, his brother, and had roomed with his sister at BYU. Stunned, I pointed to myself and indicated that I was that sister, her former roommate. The passing of more than a few years and married names had fogged our vision. We are currently planning a roommate reunion. She is still hard to contact and has not yet returned to church, but the lost and nearly forgotten have both been found. Hallelujah!

Have you ever read a story in the *Ensign* about a visiting teacher who made a difference in the first week or month of the assignment? Most stories are about that sister who came for years and made a difference through sheer diligence (and the fact that assignments didn't change too often). I know little miracles happen to new assignees, but most visiting teaching relationships take a long time to develop, and in our transitory society, that's a luxury few have. Trust takes time, even among the teachable.

LEARN FROM MY MISTAKES

ONE OF MY first visiting teaching assignments when we moved to the city was to a totally inactive sister named Rose. She lived in a run-down apartment that was furnished with crushed velvet and gilt plaster knickknacks. When I visited, I tried to ignore the omnipresent TV and the cockroaches that sometimes ran up my legs. After my first appointment, I came home and cried that a family lived in such miserable circumstances. (After I'd seen more of the city's misery, however, I had to say that Rose lived in a relatively decent place.)

I visited Rose for over a year, trying to convince myself that I was cultivating the kind of friendly relationship with her that a visiting teacher is supposed to have, but I was still very uncomfortable in her environment. I admit that I was relieved when my assignment changed and Rose was no longer on my list.

Because Rose never came to church, I didn't see her for several months. Then one day she phoned to invite me to a home decor party she was hosting—a prospect I found distasteful, given our different decorating styles.

"I haven't seen you for months!" Rose exclaimed. "How come it has been so long since you visited me?"

"Because my assignment got changed, and I'm not assigned to visit you anymore," I replied.

I regretted my words the moment I blurted them out. Tact has never been my forte, but even I recognized—albeit too late—the inexcusable thoughtlessness of what I had said. I never saw nor heard from Rose again, but I have never forgotten her because of what I learned from the stunned silence on the other end of the phone.

A BRIGHT SPOT

M Y COMPANION AND I have been visiting Sister Miller for several months. We share pleasant scriptural messages with her and always make a point of saying hello at church and at other activities. Our relationship is going well, but my favorite visit was last month when she asked me to change a bulb in the overhead fixture in her bedroom. She's short of stature and couldn't reach it herself. She lives alone, and having that light out has probably been bugging her for months. I stood on a chair, stretched up high, and accomplished the task.

She was very grateful, and we all made up jokes. How many visiting teachers does it take to change a lightbulb? Two: one to change it and one to give the message. Or how about three: one to change it, one to bring a treat, and one to call in the report. Can you think of others? It was *so* satisfying to do something really practical for her! I've been smiling all month about that!

PAYING IT FORWARD

Over the years as a visiting teacher I have struggled with turning the requirement of once-a-month visiting into something meaningful, both for me and for those I visit. Bringing a message and trying to make friends with women I have nothing in common with, often felt fake and unproductive. I have learned the importance of finding common ground and finding a way to love my visiting teachees as human beings keeps me from feeling fake.

My feelings about visiting teaching all changed for me last year when I was extremely ill and needed help from somewhere. I was hospitalized to remove a cancerous tumor and then on heavy radiation for twenty-eight treatments. During the next year I didn't feel well enough to attend meetings, or keep up with my church callings, including a service mission in our local family history center. Luckily I could be put on a leave of absence for my service mission.

But it's difficult to go on a leave of absence from household responsibilities. My visiting teachers came to the rescue. They set up a schedule to bring in three meals a week and clean my house and do my washing twice a month for six months while I struggled to regain my strength. They acted like it was no problem to perform all this service, but I know my husband and I would have starved and been wallowing in dust bunnies had they not provided this incredible service.

There is no way I can ever repay their service. I have learned to love not only my visiting teachers but the process that the Church has in place wherein we can call on and receive this kind of incredible service when we need it.

FILLING THE CALENDAR

WHEN WE LIVED in Chicago, our branch (as it was then) consisted of longtime Chicagoans, some college students, and a lot of graduate students in business or law. I'd lived in the city long enough to be a real fan of the theaters, the zoos, the museums, the lakefront, the pizza, the parks, and the El (the chaotic train that whips and squeals in an "elevated" loop around the city).

One of my visiting teaching sisters in those years of my young motherhood had a husband in a two-year graduate program. When my companion and I first went to visit her, I noticed she had a calendar in her kitchen with big red *x*'s marking off each day. She said that she missed her home out west so much and hated Chicago so much that she was counting the days until she and her husband and baby could get back home.

My companion and I took this as a challenge. We didn't want her grieving for two years. We wanted her to see what we loved about the place and to pick up on the city's delights.

We courted her with trips to the Lincoln Park Zoo with the other young moms. We gave her free tickets to local plays. We hauled her to our favorite restaurants. In December, we took her to a mall where our children had their pictures taken on the lap of a jolly black Santa.

Nothing worked. Every month we'd see those big red *x*'s marching inexorably across the weeks toward the day of her "release."

Back then I felt some resentment, I admit. She missed out on so much! She never gave the city a chance. She had a bad attitude. Our efforts were wasted.

Now, thirty years later, I would do things differently. I would stop trying to talk, walk, or "El" her out of her grief. I would talk less and listen more to her—and to the Spirit. I would share more of my stresses so she could know she wasn't as alone in her struggles as she thought. I would be more compassionate and less driven by my own agenda.

But I would still have treated her to pizza and taken her to the zoo.

PERSEVERANCE, PARKING, AND PRAYER

IN 1970, MY husband, Paul, and I were one of about a half a dozen couples who were asked to move to the single adult University Ward in Cambridge, Massachusetts, rather than attend the family Cambridge Ward when the young marrieds ward we were in was disbanded. The reason given for this move was so that we marrieds could act as "stable influence" on the singles, whatever that meant.

I was called to be a counselor in the Relief Society. We did the "full program" of the Church, even when it didn't apply to us. For instance, I was asked to teach the mother education class even though only one woman in the ward—the Relief Society president—had a child, and that baby was only six months old. Since I had no children of my own, it was like the blind leading the blind. We discussed possible scenarios about raising our future children; I've cringed many a time contemplating what I taught with such confidence about discipline and other child-rearing subjects.

Kathy, the Relief Society president, and I were visiting teaching companions, and we took all the "difficult cases" ("inactives" who didn't want to be harassed by Mormons and those living in questionable areas). Because Kathy's husband was an undergrad at Harvard, he was scarcely around to take care of their baby, so we packed baby Joy into her car seat and drove confidently into East Boston and other urban —and sometimes scary—parts of the city, day and night, since our ward encompassed all the singles in the whole Boston area.

Kathy used to pray before we left each time, partially to keep us safe but mostly to secure us a parking place. Parking in Boston has always been difficult, but at night, when career people were home from work, it was almost impossible. Every time I went visiting teaching with Kathy, we found a parking place; when trying to park on my own secular errands, I often would circle around several blocks for an hour, sometimes returning home without getting one. But we always got a parking place when I was with Kathy.

One evening, we were coming home from visiting teaching in east Boston and got lost. We thought we were getting onto Memorial Drive, the only way we knew how to get back to Cambridge (we'd both lived in the area less than a year), but we ended up on the Tobin Bridge. We were a little panicked because we didn't know where we would end up after getting off the bridge. Even worse, at that time you had pay a toll halfway across the bridge, which we hadn't realized. Neither of us had any money with us. When we saw the sign for the toll, we quickly exited into the heart of Chelsea—which might as well have been the heart of darkness for us since neither of us had ever been to Chelsea before.

At the end of the exit ramp, we pulled into a gas station and told the attendant we had gotten lost on our way to Cambridge and asked him how to get back there. He looked at us, incredulous that we had steered so off course, and then said, "Wha's a madder—youse ladies need a quaddah to get across the bridge?" And he gave us a quarter and told us how to get back to our safe little haven, Cambridge.

That experience was a great testament to the efficacy of Kathy's prayers.

The Savior calls His disciples to work with Him in His ministry, giving them the opportunity to serve others and become more like Him. In Relief Society, each sister has the opportunity to watch over and strengthen sisters one by one through visiting teaching. Sister Julie B. Beck, the fifteenth Relief Society general president, said, "Because we follow the example and teachings of Jesus Christ, we value this sacred assignment to love, know, serve, understand, teach, and minister in His behalf." — *Daughters in My Kingdom*, p. 105

MY SISTER, THE REFUGEE

IN THIS OLD dilapidated building, I followed Udori up the small, dark stairway to her tiny room on the third floor. With no air conditioning, the tropical heat added a heaviness to the afternoon. With true Asian hospitality, she offered me a glass of soda. I felt slightly guilty taking the drink, when she had so little. I had to remind myself to drink it slowly, otherwise she would fill it up again.

I was Udori's visiting teacher. She and her family were refugees from Sri Lanka, the island nation south of India. They, like all the other refugees in our ward, had come to Bangkok hoping the United Nations office that aids refugees would help them move to a third country, enabling them to start a new life. They were desperate to escape the thirty-year civil war that had ravaged their country.

Without the visiting teaching program, I never would have even met Udori, since her job (not an option for most refugees) precluded her from attending church. She had a strong testimony and regretted having to miss the church meetings. Despite the differences in our culture and background, our mutual love of the gospel sweetened our friendship. Being sisters in the gospel with a shared vision and value system gave us a closeness that I missed with my own siblings, now distanced from the Church.

Udori and I both lived in congested, downtown Bangkok. Although we were less than a mile apart, we lived in different worlds. Udori's whole family somehow managed to live together in that one small room. This was the case with every refugee family in the ward. Looking at their limited space, I wondered where everyone slept.

I tried to be as generous as possible in sharing our home and resources. I started hosting refugee events at the house including English classes, practicing church talks, sports in the yard, and always lots of food! The parents as refugees were not allowed to work, and many of their children had not yet been accepted into the very inadequate refugee school, so coming to my house was a welcome respite from their depressing circumstances. Sometimes thirty or forty people would crowd into our home, along with some American members to help. Once when I ran out of food I offered them peanut butter sandwiches, which they had never seen before, and, after eating, were not eager to try again!

In their difficult circumstances they greatly appreciated the help and support our ward gave them. It really was a rare privilege to befriend them and have them learn that regardless of status, position or nationality we are all brothers and sisters in the Gospel.

ERRANDS WITH EDITH

EDITH WAS EIGHTY-FOUR years old that muggy summer when I first met her in Maryland. She was short. I never asked her outright, but I'm guessing she could have only been five feet tall if she was standing up straight; she was a bit stooped. Her stringy gray hair was always brushed and pinned back from her face by two silver barrettes. Her hands were gnarled with age. Edith's house was more like a cabin with plywood floors. It had one bedroom that was divided from the front room by a curtain. It smelled like mothballs.

My companion, Meg, had given sufficient warning: Edith was feisty; she liked to feed the kids junk; and she needed us to visit as well as take her grocery shopping (luckily the anonymity of the phone line provided me the opportunity to make my best martyr face). Meg was unclear on all the details, only that Edith was more Catholic than she was Mormon. What she left out was that Edith was racist, would not turn off talk radio during our visits, and, that despite her frailty, she was still capable of trapping squirrels and drowning them in a bucket in her backyard.

The trips to the grocery store were grueling. I had to take both of my young children while she meandered the aisles. I tried not to rush her. I tried not to feel resentment when she would inevitably ask to stop at the dollar store while the baby screamed from the back seat. I often mentally chastised myself because I knew she had no one else. We were the only people she saw all month long. On the eve of our scheduled appointments, I would pray for a measure of charity to get me through it.

Meg moved away a few months later and left me with strict instructions to take care of Edith, as her health was rapidly deteriorating. I envied the love Meg felt for Edith, so I continued the dreaded visits, hoping my guilt would transform one of us—maybe she would go to church; maybe I would find joy in service. I began driving by her house weekly, unable to bear the thought of her dying in that tiny house alone with no one noticing.

I didn't live in Maryland long. A year later, it was time to move again, and I hounded the Relief Society president to provide me with good, capable replacement sisters. I went with them to make introductions, and Edith gave them her wary and cantankerous looks. They had kids, so I knew her heart would soften.

We said good-bye in the front yard, patches of neglected earth underneath our feet. Edith hugged my kids and gave them candy while I loaded them into my minivan. As she hobbled around the car, my heart swelled. Tears rolled down the deep lines of her face. She grabbed my waist and put her head to my chest. I hugged her back and told her the truth, "I will miss you." The strength of her grasp surprised me and I looked down at the silver barrettes, finally realizing that Edith didn't need a meetinghouse, and I didn't need to fill seats in the chapel. She needed the gospel I could give—grocery stores and rides to the doctor.

THIS LITTLE LIGHT

M Y BIGGEST CLAIM to success in visiting teaching is that we once visited a less-active woman who always kept her drapes completely closed, lights off, and always wore black. For over a year, we visit taught her in total darkness. Then, gradually, she opened the drapes a bit, turned on the lights, and once even wore a yellow shirt! She never came back to church, but maybe we turned her "light on" in a completely different way. She told us that she had never had any friends— we were the closest thing to it!

PEACE IN MY STORM

M Y NEW VISITING teacher, without a companion, sat in my apartment on the love seat. I sat on the couch nearby. I was in my twenties, married not quite two years. She was in her forties, a friendly woman who shared my interest in music and who worried little about appearances. She was the mother of six children ranging from one of the biggest teenage boys I'd ever seen to the baby she would deliver soon.

I'd had a miscarriage a few weeks before. I was weak and low, but doing my best to put a on a good face, not just for her visit, but in the successive minutes of each day, trying to smile and show outward thinking in spite of a downward, inward pull.

At some point, our friendly, light conversation turned. The Berlin Wall had just come down, and we began talking about the last days. As a child, I had been terrified of the last days. More recently, I had been thinking on all those scripture passages about how hard things would be for women who were suckling or with child. And there she was pregnant, and me having just been pregnant and wanting to be pregnant though still afraid of pregnancy and children. I was also in that tired place where small things had become big and where old, deep fears were coming up for air and flagging me down.

She talked about the last days with enthusiasm. "Wasn't it exciting?" she asked. I mentioned that I was frightened of them. She became gentler and mentioned a scripture about how in the last days, the faithful ones would be surrounded by turmoil, but it would be as if they were in the eye of the storm.

She held out faith and peace and a mother's comfort.

I don't recall if she ever visited me again, but it was enough. In that moment she was positioned in the eye of the storm, and she offered me a place there too.

CHANGE OF ROUTE

W HEN I SAW the visiting teaching coordinator roaming the halls with her "change of route" cards, I cringed. What would it mean for me . . . again? Change? Please, no change! When she finally made it to me, she handed me a card that contained a name I had never heard of. Rats!

After some sleuthing, I found that my mystery woman was young (in comparison to me) with three children under the age of five. I sighed. I was nearly an empty nester, so we would have little in common . . . again. With apprehension— and not a little dread—I made an appointment to see her one afternoon. It would take me some time to recognize that that one simple phone call made a profound difference in my life.

It turned out we did have something in common after all—money, or rather the lack of it. Her husband was a post-doctoral student and money was tight in her home as it was in mine, with a husband trying to build his own business. She felt comfortable sharing her struggles, with which I totally empathized. We spent time going to discount stores, sharing money-saving tips, and visiting garage sales on Saturday mornings. What fun my husband and I had visiting their home, tending their children, having them over for dinner, and sharing our holiday traditions with them. She and her family, who were so far away from their blood relatives, allowed me to be their surrogate mother and grandmother, which became a joy I had never felt before.

Every Sunday after sacrament meeting, when her little boy ran to give me a hug and ask if I had a small toy or piece of candy for him, my heart swelled. There was inspiration in that "change of route" card I had dreaded. Through it two unlikely women were brought together through the teachings of Christ and helped each other to make it in this challenging world.

INTERNATIONAL EXAMPLE

I READ THAT IRAQ's minister of state for women's affairs, Azhar Abdul Karem al-Sheikhly, visited the United States in 2006 specifically to spend a week in Salt Lake City, studying the Church's organization for women, the Relief Society, founded in 1842 to relieve the poor and the needy. Iraqi women have been "searching for a way to build a network that could harness their collective strength, and they discovered a remarkable model in this Mormon organization." For example, the Relief Society has visiting teachers, pairs of women assigned to visit each woman in the ward monthly and to be aware of her well-being and available to assist as needed. Azhar said, "I wish I could do this visiting teachers in my country. I wish to tell how families are strong in this country, how families take care of each other. . . . This is the way to build a new Iraq."

(Quotations from "Relief Society Intrigues Iraqi Women," by Peggy Stack, *Salt Lake Tribune*, May 27, 2006. Excerpted in *No More Goodbyes* by Carol Lynn Pearson, Pivot Point Books, 2007.)

CAROL'S TURN

I VISIT TEACH MY good friend Jill. I love doing nice things for her in the name of visiting teaching. If my partner, Carol, is in charge of setting up the appointments, I will often say, "I'll check with Jill," and then Jill, who can be honest with me, will often plead with me not to visit.

When three months of non-visiting visits stretched to four, the guilt got to me, and we made an appointment with Jill. A few hours before the scheduled visit, Jill called me and said, "You sweet sisters don't need to visit me tonight. Let's just call this good."

"Jill," I said. "Carol is planning to pick me up, so please let us come tonight, and then we'll have that taken care of for another few months." So we went to Jill's as scheduled.

No sooner had we sat down when Carol said, "Today is the anniversary of when I took my husband to the hospital." Then Carol talked about his illness and talked and talked about how close he'd come to dying. Carol needed to talk, needed to tell someone about all those things that had gone on. She needed someone to listen.

Later that evening, I called Jill and said, "I know why we came visiting teaching tonight."

Jill interrupted and said, "So Carol could talk."

Jill hadn't needed the visit, but my companion Carol had.

DELLA

W E HAD JUST returned from another overseas assignment. It was my very first Sunday at church, and they
were already giving me the names of women to visit teach. Our
family was "camping out" at our new house, waiting for our
belongings to arrive, and I already had visiting teaching assignments! Because the ward had a shortage of active women,
I was asked to visit teach without a partner. That part suited
me fine. It's always difficult to get three busy women together.

On one of those crazy evenings when I was trying to finish
up the dinner dishes and get the kids focused on their home-
work, there was another phone call. This time it was from the
Relief Society president.

"I need to find a visiting teaching companion for Della,"
she explained. Della was a recently reactivated woman in the
ward, still quite new to the Church. "I need someone who can
show her how the visiting teaching program works. It has to
be someone who can also address some of the special needs of
this sister. Although I don't know you well, your name keeps
coming to my mind. Will you accept this assignment?"

Even though part of me would have preferred to do my
visiting teaching alone, I had never felt before that a visiting teaching assignment—especially with regard to a visiting
teaching companion—was the result of such specific inspiration. Of course I agreed.

As Della and I became friends, she slowly started sharing her life story with me. Discarded as an infant, she was
raised in an abusive home. Both her biological and adoptive

mothers had failed her. She grew up fearing that perhaps God didn't love her either. Was this God's way of punishing her? Although she is a strong, resilient woman who has struggled to raise five children on her own, these fears haunted her and have contributed to a terrible lack of self-esteem.

"I have felt my whole life that I don't belong here on earth," Della once confided in me. "For years I just wanted to leave this world. I didn't seem to fit in anywhere."

"Della," I said. "I don't know why you have had such difficult circumstances throughout your life, but I do know God loves you." I told her of another Latter-day Saint woman also in an abusive family, one that she came to learn had been so for generations. A priesthood blessing she received in the midst of her trials told her she had agreed in premortal life to come to that family in order to stop the cycle of abuse.

As I told Della this story, she felt a shiver of empathy and insight. It gave her a new perspective on her circumstances that helped transform her self-image. Instead of feeling victimized and unloved, she felt empowered.

It has been incredible to see the power of the gospel change Della's life. Her faith has grown as her understanding and commitment to the gospel have grown. She continues to develop her great gift of recognizing the Spirit. I witness God at work transforming the life of my sister, friend, and visiting teaching companion, Della. I'm humbled to think God thought I could help.

JUST WHAT I NEEDED

ICALLED MY VISITING teacher Jane and told her that I really didn't feel like having them visit as we'd scheduled. "Things just aren't going well . . ." and then I started to cry and tried to quickly end our phone call. But she, a mother of ten—some of her children older than I am—interjected, "I understand. Some days are just plain hard." Later that afternoon, she delivered bagels and soup and never asked me for an explanation. That was one of the best times I was visit taught.

At the beginning of each visiting teaching relationship, ask the women you visit what they most like in their visits. Find out how long they prefer your visits to last, how often they'd like you to come, what time of day, what kind of message, if they like treats around their birthdays or holidays, if you can bring your children along. Meeting sisters' needs and wants is more easily done when you know their needs and wants.

BEYOND THE ZONE

I MET REBECCA WHILE she was attending graduate school. She was smart, beautiful, and outspoken. I was totally intimidated. I would definitely have kept my distance, but I was assigned to be her visiting teacher. It was only out of duty that I forced myself to schedule our monthly visits since she was definitely out of my comfort zone. If I had had my way, we never would have become friends. But that is the beauty of the visiting teaching program. Learning to love and serve others who are not like us increases our capacity for growth and goodness. And like many of my other visiting teaching opportunities, it changed me. Those monthly visits wore down my fears and resistance and were eventually replaced with a blossoming friendship. We have now been dear friends for thirty-five years.

HAM IN MY BACKPACK

S OMEONE DONATED A ham to the Church, thinking a family in need could use it for the holidays," says the Relief Society president on the phone shortly before Christmas. "The bishop and I agree it should go to Sister X. If we bring it to your office sometime today, could you get it to her when she gets home?"

"Sure," I reply. "I'll try."

The last few years have brought king-sized troubles in many varieties into Sister X's life. At last, her older son is out of prison, her younger son is out of the hospital, and her abusive husband is out of the house. The knife held to her throat made it easier for her to decide the marriage was over.

As her visiting teacher, I try to be supportive through it all, but it's hard to know how to help. It's even harder to show my support when it's so difficult to contact her. Although she's been in the United States for many years, she still thinks in the style of her homeland, which doesn't run on planning calendars, shall we say. Her voicemail box is full and won't accept new messages, so I just have to hope she picks up the phone. I don't think she's ever returned one of my emails, always waving it off with a laugh and a hug when I catch her in person. I know it's not personal; she just doesn't operate that way.

What does work is dropping by unannounced. If she's home, we have a nice visit, and I can see her burden lifting a little for a moment. If she's not home, I leave her a note and a trinket to let her know I'm thinking about her and that I hope things get better soon. It seems like such a small thing to do in the face of such big troubles, but it's all I can think of.

But dropping by unannounced isn't going to work with a ham.

What's worse, the ham is now in the fridge at my office, which means I'll have to deliver it on foot now that I walk to work these days. (Luckily I don't use the kosher fridge; that's in the kitchen of the department downstairs.) I can carry a five-pound ham in my backpack no problem, but I don't want to carry it back and forth for days hoping to catch her at home. Surely she'll respond to my voicemails and emails this time, knowing there's a free ham riding on it.

After two days of unanswered phone calls and emails, I think of a new technique. I mail her a letter. A postage stamp probably never traveled a shorter distance in the history of the

US Postal Service. Two days later, still no response. Maybe she doesn't like ham.

I load up the backpack and sling the five-pound ham onto my shoulders. With the Relief Society president's permission, I stop at the house of Sister Y, whose recent challenges rival Sister X's. Her husband's store just got robbed for the second time in three months, and they fear for their lives as well as their livelihood. I step inside her door, slip off my backpack and pull out the ham. "Merry Christmas, Sister Y."

"[Jesus Christ] showed us how to minister— how to watch over and strengthen one another. His was a ministry to individuals, one by one." —*Daughters in My Kingdom,* p. 105

ASK!

WHAT AM I doing to help my sisters feel that I am a friend who loves and cares for them? How can I become better at watching over and caring for others?

My answer to both of these questions is this: *Ask the women you visit teach.* It is quite clear in these questions that the message is not for you just to hand out to the women you visit, but that it is preparatory material for the you, the teacher, to use to developing trusting friendships with the women you visit teach. Rather than reciting the formal monthly visiting teaching message verbatim as the "gospel message," I see no wrong in seeking inspiration for what is personally best for the individual sisters.

WHAT I LIKE, WANT, AND NEED

"I like it when my visiting teachers bring me treats."

"Please don't bring little goodies when you come to visit me. I don't need doodads, and I'm trying to watch my weight, so having food around is just a temptation."

"If you really want to meet my needs, arrange a sitter for any child older than a babe-in-arms. I feel too distracted otherwise. I get worn out enough by my own kids."

"I love to have you bring your kids along. They bring life into the house. I can bring out the grandkids' toys or pop a short video in to keep them happy, and we can have a wonderful visit. I remember how hard it is for young mothers to get done what they want and need to when they have little ones."

"As a working sister, I would much prefer a phone call or a

drop off treat to a sit down visit. I enjoy visiting while my visiting teachers are actually here, but after they leave I sometimes feel the panic of all I didn't get done during that time."

RELIEF, SOCIETY

I'M TOO POOR to work out at the snooty athletic clubs near my house, and too old and pudgy to work out at Bally's or Gold's, so I go to the YMCA with all the other middle-aged mommies trying to sneak in thirty minutes on the Stairmaster while their kids take swimming lessons. The particular YMCA I go to is also home of the legendary 9:00 a.m. MWF Aquacise class.

The median age of the women in this class is, I'd guess, around seventy-five. All of the women are pretty spry, still fit enough to get themselves to the pool and into the water for forty-five minutes of foam-floating-device-assisted water aerobics. I often end up showering and changing at the same time as they finish class—in fact, lately I've been working out longer than I usually would to make sure I'm in the locker room when they are. I love watching and listening to them.

As far as I can tell, they have few things in common, besides their commitment to exercise and to each other. I've heard a few pointed political comments that suggest divergent views; there's talk of the different churches and synagogues they attend; some have been to college, some not; some are widowed, some still married, one or two divorced. Their bodies are every size and shape imaginable—tall, short, round, lumpy, thin, saggy, wiry, scarred, varicose, stretch-marked, well-muscled, well-used, all with that softly loosening skin of the aged. All of them seem beautiful to me.

The core members of this group have been taking the same class for nearly a decade. On Wednesdays after class they have brunch together, either at someone's home or at a local diner. They have seen each other through the loss of spouses, cancer diagnoses and treatments, sending grandsons to Iraq, births of grandchildren (and a few "greats"), moves to assisted living facilities. They keep track of class members who have moved away or gone to Florida for the winter, posting notes and cards on a bulletin board in the locker room. When one woman didn't reappear in class after what the ladies considered a suitable period of mourning after her husband's death, they organized a posse to visit her, get her to eat, and coax her back into the routine of exercise classes.

What is most interesting to me about this community is that what binds them is not some lofty shared ideal, but simply a series of decisions to care for each other. Over time, those small choices—to have a conversation after class, to share a meal, to divulge a secret, to ask for or offer a ride to the doctor's office—have built sturdy and lasting friendships on a foundation as flimsy as, well, a swimming pool.

I often chafe at the assigned and enforced friendships of visiting teaching, longed for some more "authentic" community. I don't imagine I'm finished with those frustrations, but for now, I'm learning from the little old ladies in the locker room to love and appreciate a female relief society on a more human scale, to recognize and savor the gifts that come from simply choosing to tend each other, body and soul.

"My desire is to plead with our sisters to stop worrying about a phone call or a quarterly or monthly visit, and whether that will do, and concentrate instead on nurturing tender souls." —Mary Ellen Smoot, in *Daughters in My Kingdom*, p. 117

TRUST ISSUES

NOT ALL OF us are in a place in our lives where we have the ability to claim perfect revelation in regard to anyone, including ourselves, and especially to the women we visit teach. When we truly desire to serve with a sincere heart, the sisters we teach will know. To me, this means listening, being a sounding board, and not judging.

From a practical perspective, I also believe that this includes regular, real contact. I say this as a person with trust issues. It takes me a good six months or more (or never) for me to trust some people. Okay, a lot of people. The people who I have come to trust, for the most part, are those who I have regular communication with. For example:

Visiting teacher A used to tick off the "made contact" box if she saw me at church. I resented this, and although I was desperately struggling at the time, her choice to tick me off the list made me not want to have her visit me.

Visiting teacher B stopped by to talk "at" me; she did not

listen, she did not know me, and she gossiped about other church members in our visits. I still do not trust her.

Visiting teacher C came to my home and shared a message. I said that I could not apply the message in my life right then, and I didn't think it related to me. She patiently listened to my issue, and agreed that I needed to do what was right for me—which was *not* the stock message! She then asked me how she could support me in that. To this day, I am in touch with her, and I would do nearly anything for her. This beloved friend really taught me how to be a visiting teacher and a woman of faith. I trust her with my life.

IT WORKED FOR US

O NE OF MY all-time favorite visiting teachers was a sister who never once made a visit or even a phone call.

She loved tole painting and was very creative. I had her as my visiting teacher for only three months—October, November, and December. Each of those months I found on my doorstep a necklace that she made for me to wear to school: a pumpkin necklace, a turkey necklace, and a Santa necklace—invaluable for first grade teaching. My only regret is that she couldn't be my visiting teacher longer because I would have loved an Easter necklace. Her doing visiting teaching the way it was fun for her made it fun for me.

ELEVATED AIMS

Eliza R. Snow, second Relief Society general president, taught: "Paul the Apostle anciently spoke of holy women. It is the duty of each one of us to be a holy woman. We shall have elevated aims, if we are holy women. We shall feel that we are called to perform important duties. No one is exempt from them. There is no sister so isolated, and her sphere so narrow but what she can do a great deal towards establishing the Kingdom of God upon the earth" ("A Society of Holy Women," *Ensign*, August 2011).

What are the elevated aims that you share with the sisters you visit teach? Do you share a strong bond in regard to educating children? Find some fun, educational websites to share! Do you share a desire to help impoverished women? Discover and discuss micro loans or women's shelters. Are you closet foodies? Compare pesto recipes. You know you love pesto!

Seek something in which you can develop true friendship, which can develop further into the bond shared between holy women. This is sisterhood.

THE MOVE-IN & ME

One summer, several families moved out of our ward and several others moved in. Among the move-outs was a woman on my visiting teaching route, so I expected a change in my assignment. As new sisters were introduced in Relief Society one Sunday, I began wondering which of them I might be asked to visit.

Seated on the front row was a young mother who seemed cheerful, excited about moving to our area, and ready to serve in a new ward. Seated in a back corner was another young mother with a dour expression who seemed—at best—resigned to her new situation and the necessity of dealing with new people. I knew that the cheerful woman lived fairly close to me, so I hoped the Relief Society president would put her on my list.

You can guess which one I was assigned to visit. I was disappointed at first; but during my first visit with the dour-looking sister, I began to understand why she looked the way she did, and why she seemed less than excited about moving to our area. I did the best I could to alleviate her fears and help her feel comfortable in our ward. As we became better acquainted, I learned that we had much in common.

Soon I began to look forward to our visits rather than dread them. By opening our minds and hearts to one another during those visits, we eventually became very good friends.

DELIGHTING IN
THE DETAILS

I FINALLY FOUND A way to make visiting teaching fun for me. I work, my partner works, and the sisters we visit work. So my partner and I only make sit-down visits giving an actual lesson every three months. During the off months, we take turns dropping by our sisters' homes with a treat. Those treats make me actually think about my sisters more often than I probably would if I were doing monthly sit-down visits. When I am out shopping I often think, "That would be fun to take to Pam and Sue."

The things I drop off are simple, inexpensive, and usually things I would like someone to bring to me. I've taken a Ziploc bag of almonds, a grocery store shamrock plant, a couple of daffodils, a small bowl of fresh raspberries, some health bars for them to take in their car for snacks, a container of almond butter, room freshener, soup from a maxi-mart, and once in a rare while something I have actually baked. Doing visiting teaching this way makes it less of a chore and more creative and loving on my part.

CULTURE CLASHES

Cultural differences in the worldwide Church don't always do us favors. For example, when I was eighteen, I moved to Utah for school. My father died in the middle of my first year there. It was expected; he had cancer. But I was far from home and naïve when struck with the reality of death. I found myself struggling deeply with his death, with Utah culture, and with the distance from home.

One winter afternoon, the student ward Relief Society presidency came to our apartment. I answered the door, and they asked to speak to my roommate, so I made myself scarce. After they left, my roommate told me that they had come to offer their condolences to me.

Huh? I was right there, and they asked to speak to my roommate? About me? Now, I know in part this situation was tainted by youth and inexperience, and I also have come to the conclusion that the Relief Society presidency was trying to be respectful. Or at least they stuck to a cultural pattern that they thought was correct.

But I grew up in New York. And in my newly-graduated-from-high-school mind, I still clung to the idea that when someone talks about you behind your back, you are supposed to beat them up. So you do not talk about people. At all. That's what you call gossip. You talk *to* people face to face. But the Relief Society presidency—as a group—talked to my roommate about me.

Rest assured, I've never been in a physical fight (outside of childhood sibling skirmishes), and I would never have gone to the Relief Society president's dorm and started swinging punches. But cultural differences made me believe that I was being gossiped about, and left me with a bitter and distrustful introduction to Relief Society that still haunts me today. So visiting teaching is hard because we are a global church, because we are from different families and because we hope and expect different things when communicating.

A CAUTIONARY TALE

HERE IS A visiting teaching cautionary tale. When I was a young mother with two little bundles of joy, I was also commuting between two universities, taking courses at both. My husband was a management consultant and on the road frequently. My house was a complete mess, and the elders quorum was having a social at our place on Friday. My visiting teachers really wanted to get 100 percent that month and just had to see me on Friday, my only day to clean. I said, "Fine, but bring your rubber gloves and come ready to work because I'm swamped, and I can't really afford the time on that particular day."

To my absolutely amazement, they came, ignored the disarray, sat in my living room and gave their carefully prepared message (on charity, I think). Even with fairly large hints, my situation was lost on them.

The result of their visit is that they taught me to be a better observer and listener in visiting teaching and in life. Not a bad lesson for anyone.

WHY I LOVE VISITING TEACHING

I'M A FAN of visiting teaching. I've been doing it all my life. My mom was the eternal Relief Society president and, with me as her underage companion, she assigned us to visit people who didn't really want to be visited. But we always got in, often with the help of cookies, and usually ended up making nice connections.

In my current ward, they just rearranged the assignments and I have a GLS companion (Good Little Soldier). Which is great. Except that one of the women we teach is a physician who calls it like she sees it (let's call her OMD, Outspoken MD). So I've been visiting her on the sly because I'm a chicken and was afraid to bring my GLS along. But this month, we had a traditional visit. Here's what happened.

We sit and chat for a while and things go well until GLS says it's time for the Message. Before she can even open the *Ensign* OMD says politely but firmly, "Let me stop you right there. Is the lesson on prayer and faith and love?"

GLS looks confused, "Why yes, have you already read it?"

OMD sighs. "No. But all the lessons are on prayer and faith and love. These lessons don't work for me. I don't find any useful religion in them."

There ensued a very awkward silence.

Luckily I remembered a thought I'd had earlier that day and shared it as my message. I told both women that I struggle as a Young Women teacher and as a mom with lots of the stories in manuals and magazines. I want to promote faith but fear that presenting only the "and everything got fixed" version of life was dangerous. The gospel is *not* an insurance policy against pain and suffering; but it is the best tool I have in my arsenal to deal with life in the real world.

I was surprised when GLS agreed with me and shared a hard story about her mom getting cancer, twice, and her sister leaving the Church because she felt God had betrayed the family by not keeping the cancer away.

OMD talked about how she was strengthened by the faith of one of her patients, a man she'd helped perform a liver transplant on the night before. He was eighty pounds, had contracted hepatitis C from a blood transfusion as a kid, and had been in excruciating liver failure for a while. She marveled at his optimism, his gratitude, and his refusal to live life as if he had a death sentence, which he basically did. That was where she found her faith.

We all talked and laughed, and I was so thankful that OMD spoke up and told us what she needed. And I was even more thankful that GLS was not offended but was willing to share her personal message of prayer and faith and love as well.

I need to remember that just because someone toes the line and follows rules doesn't mean they can't be flexible when necessary. And just because someone says they don't believe in visiting teaching doesn't mean they can't use a good conversation with friends at least once a month.

Part of the challenge is to keep visiting teaching from becoming one more obligation and one more pressure. How do we do that? One way is to share insight and inspiration with each other. When we see how flexibility, faith, creativity, consistency, and good humor help others, we are bolstered as well.

RECIPROCITY

THOSE OF US who darken the doors of Latter-day Saint chapels know how to be good visiting teachers. We hear the lessons often enough. What we don't hear is how to be good visiting teachees. The other side of all that service we are instructed to render is that we must also be on the receiving side. We must be the gracious recipients of all the kindly gestures that others make towards us. Teachees must be available to fit their visitors' schedules; they must put aside other activities to listen to presentations; they must bite their tongues and not object to the lessons; they must prepare their children for the destruction of their rooms by young visitors.

But teachees can also be proactive. They can teach their teachers. We get to know these people pretty well and can observe their problems, even as they observe ours.

Sometimes they ask for our help. Sometimes we can see clearly just what they need and provide it for them.

Another useful teachee strategy is to think of our visiting teachers as people who feel bound to help us. Often I have projects that require some committee assistance but which are outside of regular Church channels. I call on my visiting teachers and ask them to help me out. My pitch is that besides the fact that I will be eternally grateful for their help, they can count it as a visit.

I also ask for help from my own teachees. They don't feel as honor-bound to help me out as my own visiting teachers, but we still form a special unit of mutual assistance. Back and forth, up and down. It is in these little cells of mutual cooperation that we can become real friends.

RIGHT PLACE, RIGHT TIME

W HEN WE MOVED to northern Virginia, I was assigned to visit teach Tran, a Vietnamese sister. She had been less active so long that her contact information was incomplete. It took some time to track her down. Although born in Vietnam, it turned out she was ethnically Chinese. With the worldwide diaspora, Chinese are everywhere. This was fortunate, since her English was limited. We communicated with my not-great-but-manageable Chinese, although her thick Vietnamese accent made her hard for me to understand.

When her grown son Vu arrived home, he helped interpret when I got stuck. He was working as a bouncer at a bar—a surprising job for an LDS guy who wasn't very big. Besides trying to come back to church, he was also looking for a new job. He explained that his options were limited since his sister had totaled his car, and he now had to rely on public transportation.

The next week when an Asian-American plumber arrived at the house to fix our shower faucet, I asked him about his job. He was an immigrant who had been trained by his company. And, yes, a new job had recently opened. He gave me the inside scoop and told me how to proceed. I immediately called Vu and passed along the information. He was thrilled with the job prospect and discovered a bus close to his apartment that went directly to the company. I even drove him over for the job interview. We were both delighted when he got the job! I certainly saw God's hand in that surprising development. I hope Vu did too. It was another unexpected blessing from visiting teaching.

LESSONS AND LAUNDRY

ENTERING THE LADIES' room at church one morning between Sunday school and Relief Society, I found Megan and her baby daughter in the midst of a diapering disaster. The baby must have had a bout of diarrhea because her clothes were a mess, and the front of Megan's dress looked even worse. My horror at Megan's predicament increased when I realized that this sobbing, wretched woman was supposed to teach the Relief Society lesson in only a few minutes.

Before I could muster enough presence of mind to offer to

lead the sisters in hymns or something while Megan cleaned herself up, Claire, Megan's visiting teacher, rushed into the bathroom.

"I heard what happened," Claire said. "Don't worry. I've got this all figured out. Here, you hold the baby. Now, Megan. Take off that dress."

As soon as she had shoved Megan's baby into my arms, Claire began unzipping her own dress. "Don't just stand there, Megan!" she ordered. "Take off your dress! Relief Society is about to start!"

As I stood there gaping, Claire handed Megan her own outfit, then took Megan's soiled one and put it on. "There," she said. "Don't worry about the baby. I'll take her home. Now go teach your lesson."

I don't remember the lesson that Megan taught in Relief Society that morning, but I'll always remember the one that Claire taught in the bathroom.

AWED BY HELPING HANDS

I WAS A VISITING teaching companion to either Sister Thomas or Sister Shore, depending on who was available, in our ward on Chicago's South Side. These two women were older, single women, longtime residents of the city, and fairly recent converts to the Church. We were assigned to visit an elderly sister who never got to church.

One time when I was with Sister Shore, we waded through a yard filled with dog droppings and debris to find this sister alone in a filthy home. We asked what we could do. She said she wanted to wash her hair. Sister Shore lovingly washed, dried, and combed this sister's hair while I watched in awe.

Another time when Sister Thomas and I were together, the elderly sister complained that her legs hurt, and she couldn't get around or to church. Sister Thomas went down on her knees and rubbed the sister's legs, all the while praying that they would be able to bear her weight and allow her to get around. I was so reminded of the sisters at Winter Quarters and the support they gave each other, yet this time it was two visiting teachers showing that same understanding of the gospel.

POODLES AND PONDERING

SATURDAY MORNING, ONE of the women on my new visiting teaching list called. She's in her mid-fifties, a well-educated widow, and an in-again-out-again church attender (currently in one of her "in again" modes) with a car of her own.

"Can you take my dog and me to the vet?" she asked. "Fifi's been scratching her ears, and I'm just sure she's got an ear infection. My car's working fine, but could you drive? I'd just feel better that way, you know, if I can hold Fifi."

"Um, well, okay," I stammered. "When is the appointment?"

"I'll call you back after the vet tells me what time to bring her in," she said and hung up.

I put the phone down feeling grumpy and manipulated. Why had I said yes? Should I really be accompanying a mature woman and her dog to the vet? At what point does providing service interfere with encouraging self-reliance? Now I'd tied up my morning—and my family's —waiting for further word. And then who knew how the day would have to be restructured to work around poor Fifi's worrisome ears?

I paced and fumed. I could hear a little angel and a little devil on my shoulders whispering their conflicting counsel. The problem was I couldn't tell which counsel was from whom.

"She's lonely and concerned about her pooch! She needs your help!"

"Take a woman to the vet and she learns to use you as a taxi service; teach a woman to take herself to the vet and she becomes a contributing member of society."

"When ye have done it unto one of the least of these—even Fifi . . ."

"So your whole family should call your visiting teacher to get them where they need to be because you're off helping this lady and her poodle?"

Finally, muttering about this to my best friend, I said, "I'm really just trying to be like Jesus like the song says, but I don't know what that is in this situation. I don't think He'd be as conflicted as I am."

My friend's response was quick. "You already told her you'd take her. Regardless of how Jesus would make his decision, I think that once He said He'd help, He wouldn't whine. He'd just do it."

As it turned out, the vet wasn't taking "patients" at all that day. I was spared the trip but granted a lesson: Think, ponder, pray, decide . . . and once decided, stop whining.

If someone you teach has severe, complicated, or multiple problems, make sure you tell the Relief Society president. Don't gossip about these issues and avoid getting consumed by them. You are there to be a help and a support to the sister—not a loan broker, social worker, therapist, confessor, real estate agent, attorney, nag, cure-all, or doormat.

SISTER SARA AND THE BACK STORY

MANY PEOPLE WERE afraid of my mom as she became increasingly infirm, unable to walk, and needing help with most daily routines. Not so with Sara. As my visiting teacher, she gladly came whenever I called on her for help. This happened during times when I had emergencies at work and couldn't get home to take care of Mom's needs. As a young, newly married college student, Sara was wiser than her years. In my most desperate times, feeling pulled between a full-time job and taking care of Mom at home, I could count on Sara. She would come at a moment's notice like a guardian angel. Always cheerful and very gentle with me and my mom, she never winced at helping Mom get to the bathroom and seemed to take these delicate needs in stride.

Sara's selfless and sensitive service would have been enough, but there was another part to this story that really taught me a lesson.

A few years earlier, before I took Mom into my care, I had a serious conflict with Sara's parents. At the time, our church callings brought us together under some trying circumstances, and conflicts erupted between a group of ward and stake leaders, the likes of which I had never seen before or since. A few years passed, and those tensions eventually subsided. Sara's family moved to a faraway city, and I never expected to see them again.

I'm ashamed to say I would never have chosen Sara as my visiting teacher because of the distance created by those historical conflicts. What a loss that would have been! How small and petty I felt when she became such an enormous help to my family. It seemed so ironic that she and her husband would unwittingly end up in my ward. She would have been a youth at the time of the controversies, and, to this day, I have no idea whether she actually knew about them.

However, I clearly remember the day that her parents came to visit our ward after a few years had passed. I put my arm around her father and told him what a lifesaver Sara had been and how grateful I was for her goodness to us. I thanked him for sharing his family with our ward and expressed my love for him and his wife. Tears streamed down his face. We both understood the grand design and blessing that had come from Sara's innocent service.

From that moment, I saw more clearly that there really are no good guys or bad guys in the dramas of our church callings. For the most part, we all bring our baggage to the altar of service. The Lord has set it up so that when we trip, someone will ultimately come along to catch us. In my case, a beautiful spirit named Sara unknowingly lifted my family up and brought all of us out from behind enemy lines in the process.

As a young, humble visiting teacher, Sara was not only lifesaving, but also soul-saving for me.

JEAN'S JOURNEY

JEAN LOOKED LIKE she had it all together. She was married, had a full-time job, and a grown daughter. She was also branch Relief Society president. She'd been invited to speak at a major Latter-day Saint conference and to meet the General Relief Society Presidency.

Things were not as they appeared.

Jean's husband was a drug dealer and user and couldn't keep a job. Her own job, which was emotionally satisfying, paid next to nothing. Just before flying off to speak at the conference, Jean and a friend from the branch converted to the Church of Wealth and Power. They attended our church Sunday mornings and that church Sunday afternoons. The Church of Wealth and Power's charismatic bishop promised Jean she'd be a millionaire and a prophetess if she paid him a 15-percent tithe.

While teaching Relief Society, Jean bore her testimony of the new church and passed out a healing oil bought from her new bishop. The branch president released Jean from her Relief Society calling, and she was very offended.

Her hurt and anger swelled, and she stopped coming to Church. Visiting teachers encouraged her to rejoin her sisters at the branch, but they were unsuccessful. She was sure she would become a millionaire. She paid so much tithing to the Church of Wealth and Power that she and her husband were evicted and had to move into a condemned house outside the branch boundaries. She did not let sisters from the new branch come visit her. Occasionally she talked to one of her old visiting teachers—me—and one friend from her old branch.

I happened to be in Salt Lake and bought Jean a book autographed by one of Jean's favorite LDS authors. When I got back, Jean happily accepted the book. Her heart softened a tiny bit. She allowed visiting teachers from the new branch to come. They loved her into attending church. She is now back to full activity in her branch, has a job in the Relief Society, and has finally divorced the drug dealer.

Now her life is really beginning to look good.

PERSPECTIVES

THIS MONTH'S LESSON is about living within our means, and it's my turn to teach. At Claudia's house I make my way across the still-marked-from-the-vacuum pink carpet to her white couch. To my right is a display case full of Lladro figurines. I have consistently refused her suggestion of bringing my two-year-old along visiting teaching with me. I worry enough about me losing my balance and crashing into something irreplaceable in her house.

I talk about debt. About what a blessing it is to get out of it. I share a personal story about how just last month, after two years of planning and scrimping, we finally paid off everything that we accrued in the first two years of our marriage while we fixed up our house. Claudia looks at me intently and agrees that yes, it is nice to be financially "free." Her tall teenage daughter comes in and asks for the keys to the car. Since my "means" and Claudia's are so incredibly different, and I certainly don't have any financial wisdom to offer Claudia, I am starting to wish that I would have chosen a different angle for the lesson.

But perhaps this is the magic of visiting teaching: the opportunity it gives us to see things from different perspectives. Perspectives we might not see otherwise. Perspectives we might even shy away from. Because I am a visiting teacher, I am reminded that I might someday have carpet where the vacuum marks last and a daughter who is old enough to drive. Claudia's life probably hasn't always been pink and plush, and as I give the lesson, she may be remembering things she has forgotten.

NEVER FAILETH

FOR YEARS I had been half expecting the phone call, but it still brought a jolt when it came: Thelma was in the hospital, expected to die within days.

I was Thelma's visiting teacher. Although she wasn't a member of the Church, sending sisters to her home was a tradition in our ward. Her home was half a block from mine, but I had never seen her before I made my first, companionless visit.

Due to advanced age and fragile health, Thelma spent her days hunched in her worn beige armchair. Her companions were her television set and her tray full of craft supplies—sequins, styrofoam balls, popsicle sticks, glue guns. Her only kin were hundreds of miles away.

In the beginning, making conversation was difficult. She and I had little in common, and she didn't want to hear any preaching. "I'll talk about anything except politics and religion," she'd quip. I'd do my best to keep the chit-chat going and keep my toddler out of her craft basket. After putting in my hour, I'd walk away with a sigh of relief.

Yet my sense of duty kept me coming back. Thelma never complained about being lonely, but whenever I knocked on her door she would look up with a hungry expression. I felt compelled to visit her every few weeks. As the months passed, I enjoyed her company more. Rather than scrounging for small talk, we were able to pick up threads of past conversations and continue them. She grew fond of my children, and I grew fond of finding small ways to delight her. One Christmas Eve I nearly burst with anticipation as I carried a surprise treat to her door: a pineapple upside-down cake, the dessert she had prepared for her family every yuletide in years past.

Still, every time I followed the sidewalk back to my own home, a part of me was glad to leave Thelma's dull, small world behind—and for that, I felt guilty. Of course, I had my own life to attend to, and Thelma's need for companionship was a deep chasm that I could not fill on my own. Although I cared about her, I feared I was failing to truly love her. If I loved her, I told myself, I would wish I could stay longer.

After hearing of Thelma's hospitalization, I rushed over to see her. And yet as I walked toward her hospital room with the knowledge that this visit would be our last, I felt the same relief, the same guilt, the same heaviness of failure.

Her neighbor stopped me outside the closed door. "It's not pretty in there," she warned.

Walking in, I saw Thelma on the hospital bed, twisted into an unnatural position, her limbs contorted and her neck craned backward. Her face was covered by an oxygen mask. Her breathing was shallow and rapid.

I approached her with forced cheerfulness. "Hi, Thelma!" I said, reaching out my hand. I didn't think she was conscious, but as soon as she felt my touch, her hand immediately grasped mine with surprising firmness. Her touch was urgent, earnest; her vulnerability filled the air between us. How frightened she must have been.

Awash in emotion, my selfish, mortal perspective melted away. I felt Thelma's beauty, her power, her preciousness. Our many differences—age, interests, faith—disappeared. What remained was the bond between two sisters, a connection that had been secretly forming an hour at a time, a thought at a time, a choice at a time. I was overcome with surprise, and with gratitude.

Sincerity swelled within me, nearly choking me, as I told Thelma I loved her and thanked her for being part of my life. I could barely hear her response, muffled by the oxygen mask covering her face, but I didn't need to. She was thanking me, telling me she loved me too.

Walking away from her for the last time, I wished neither of us had to go.

I'll never forget the love that filled me that afternoon. It was so easy, so clear, so true—so different from what I usually feel. Often my efforts to love others feel like hard work. And while my intentions are usually good, rarely do they feel pure. Mixed up with my sincere desires to help, lift, and serve others is all the pride, laziness, and selfishness of my mortal self. My connection with the peaceful, constant love of Christ feels erratic at best. I usually—and mistakenly—conclude that the love I feel is horribly tainted, or that it doesn't "count," or that it's not even real.

No matter what connection we seek it seems that our fallen natures always get in the way somehow. Charity does not suddenly appear in dramatic deathbed scenes. Rather, it grows quietly within us, accumulating bit by bit through our daily thoughts and words and acts, slowly transforming us. Yes, the change is mostly invisible, cloaked in our busy, messy, flawed mortal lives and selves. But it is real.

I rejoice in the truth that God's love is great enough to absorb our weaknesses, heal our wounds, fill our hearts and make us one. Our hold on divinity may waver, but the divine hold on us is steady. Our attempts at charity may even seem to fail, but God's never will.

My maternal grandmother helped create my belief of what visiting teaching is supposed to be. She would reminisce, after she was housebound, about how wonderful it was to actually go into another woman's home, "You get to know a person in their home in ways that you wouldn't otherwise get to know them."

KEEPING CONNECTED

IN AN EXCLUSIVE area of town, Nancy lived in a beautiful, big home decorated superbly and filled with many treasures. She also had problems—physical and emotional—and an abusive husband. Her conversion to the gospel of Jesus Christ brought great joy and an outlet to share her many talents. However, she would periodically spiral into reclusive depressions as she felt her life could not measure up to the happiness she perceived in other families.

I was assigned as her visiting teacher. For some of the time, I visited with a partner, but for long periods Nancy would request no visits or Church contact. I continued on my own to find reasons for contact—seeking her advise about furniture polish, discussing our teenagers, whatever would allow access. As time passed, we became good friends.

During her separation and divorce process from her husband, Nancy accepted our invitation to Sunday dinner. Ed, a new member of our ward in similar circumstances, was also brave enough to join our exuberant brood. Cupid must have joined our six children's scheming, because before long, wedding plans ensued for Ed and Nancy.

Due to circumstances, typical parties were problematic, so while Ed and Nancy were away on their honeymoon, several other sisters and I gave them a surprise for their return. We toilet-papered the interior of their entire elegant home (using only the best coordinating designer toilet paper, of course)! We scattered hearts, tied balloons and left wrapped assorted rice items and our wedding gift. They loved our celebration and even left it intact for several weeks.

I believe Nancy and I grew to understand the message of love, which was both given and gratefully received through the years. Visiting teaching is always a two-way street.

A MISSED OPPORTUNITY

LAUREN WAS MY visiting teacher who never came to see me and never called. Aside from ruining the Relief Society statistics, I really didn't mind. But there was something different about Lauren. I kept having a small but insistent feeling that I should call her. I resisted. Wasn't she supposed to call me? We were both Americans living in Taipei, Taiwan. She was single, in her late thirties, and working as a teacher at the international school.

On our last night in Taiwan, while packing my bags to move the next day, I finally called Lauren. What a shame I had waited so long! I discovered she had come from a divorced home and had an irresponsible dad. She didn't trust men and struggled with depression. Still single, she felt betrayed by God, who she considered one more questionable "male" in her life. I could relate to all of it. With a few minor differences, it was the story of my life.

I had managed to work through the issues and move on. She was still stuck. Now I understood why Heavenly Father had repeatedly been asking me to call her. It would have been so easy to help her. I so regretted my unwillingness to listen to God's promptings. I had missed the opportunity to make a difference in someone's life. I told Lauren I really wanted to keep in touch and be a support to her, but she never responded to any of my efforts.

God sometimes gives us unique opportunities to change people's lives. I now pay more attention to those spiritual promptings. I don't want to miss another opportunity to help when God needs me.

VISITING VONNY

I THOUGHT WE COULD go and visit some of the elderly ladies in the ward," said my new visiting teaching companion. My heart dropped. As a newlywed immigrant without children, I craved the company of women who were closer to me in age.

My new companion was a grandmother, and all of

the women we visited were grandmothers, or even great-grandmothers. They had all lived in the area for multiple decades; two were elderly enough that they were no longer able to attend Church. All of these women were lovely, but their generational entrenchment left me with a deep sense of loneliness.

Still, I was determined to do this assignment, more for my reputation than for my soul. My companion and the first two women we visited had known each other for years and chatted together as old friends. The room seemed to fall silent when I spoke, like an intruder who did not belong. I left with a distinct sense of incompatibility.

The last woman we visited was different. Vonny was in a nursing home and suffered from dementia. I was not familiar with dementia and quickly felt silly for trying to share the assigned message. She seemed to know my companion, but she was uneasy about me. In the end, we shared thoughts on handsome actors. She thought the actors contemporary; I placed them as classic actors from the 1930s black and white film era.

The nursing home was walking distance from my house, which was unusual given the generous ward boundaries. I often went past it when walking my dog in the morning, so I decided that I would visit Vonny once a week or more. I rationalized that if she were able to recognize me, then I could consider this assignment a success.

Each time I visited her, I started by telling her my name. Even though I clearly had a foreign accent, and told her my husband was a recent convert, she spent the entire visit trying to place me within the well-rooted families in the area. Unable to do so, the meetings were frustrating for both of us. I felt as though my visiting her was doing more harm than good, but the nurses at the nurse at the front desk always warmly thanked me for visiting.

"If I only had a gimmick," I thought, "that would trigger her to recognize me. . . ." I made a query about bringing my dog, Mo, with me to the nursing home. The administrators of the nursing home were thrilled, and suggested that many of the residents would love a visit from a dog. With that, I registered Mo and myself as official visitors at the nursing home. In just a couple of weeks after the application and supply of Mo's vaccination and training records, we became official nursing home volunteer visitors.

As I walked through the halls of the nursing home with Mo for the first time, residents would call out from their rooms. Many of them kept dog treats in their nightstands, hoping for a canine visitor. We happily stopped by all of the rooms in Vonny's wing with licks, tail wags, and occasionally even a hug and a kiss from me. This early interaction convinced me that Vonny would recognize and remember my large, friendly Labrador—and therefore, me. I saved Vonny's room for last, planning to savor the time with her and my very special— though unofficial—visiting teaching companion.

Vonny jumped in her bed when she saw us.

"I am afraid of dogs!" Her panicked look mimicked her words, "No, no, no, no, no . . . !" We left immediately.

I went home feeling utterly stupid. Because she had been incoherent at our visits, it never occurred to me to ask Vonny if she liked dogs. And now I was committed to visit the nursing home with Mo. It seemed like the harder I tried, the more the situation became time-consuming and difficult.

I decided to take stock of the situation. Vonny was not very flexible. In fact, she hardly moved at all. So unless I pointed him out, I could likely bring Mo into her room and say hello to her. That way, I could do a sort of quick, token visit, before going to the other residents on her floor who were happy with a furry visitor. I also conceded that it was unlikely Vonny would ever recall or even notice me, so I decided to remove myself.

I would be a nameless, forgotten visiting teacher. That would have to suffice.

The next time I went to visit Vonny, I made sure Mo stayed out of her line of sight. "Hi, Vonny," I said. "I am your visiting teacher."

"Hello!" Vonny responded more vibrantly that she had previously. I was surprised, but decided to go with the flow. "How about a prayer?" I asked.

Vonny folded her arms and bowed her head, something she had never done before. After I prayed, I asked Vonny a question that was simple, just to see if she would respond. A miraculous flood of words came from her unlike anything she had spoken before. She told me of her mission, of visiting teaching, and of her father. After such a golden outpouring, I was content, so left and visited some other people on her floor. On the way out, I decided to call into her room again. Once again, I did not say my name, but introduced myself as her visiting teacher. Though she did not recall that I was there just twenty minutes before, she again responded to my "visiting teacher" introduction. We shared a prayer, and I went home.

I was amazed. Vonny didn't know *me*—but she knew visiting teaching! Visiting teaching wasn't about me doing a cute, clever, or even an efficient job. In this situation, it was not about me sharing a message. This assignment had nothing to do with me at all.

Or did it?

The truth was, that although her body and mind were wracked by dementia, Vonny taught *me*. She taught me about being a visiting teacher. I learned that by removing everything that distinguished me as an individual, true charity was expressed through the unadulterated act of being a nameless visiting teacher.

In the next few months, I continued to visit Vonny, usually without Mo. I never told her my name, and always introduced myself as her visiting teacher. She always bowed her head when I offered a prayer, and on her better days, she even shared her thoughts on scriptures that I read to her.

Although I normally visited Vonny on my own, my companion was able to join me on a final visit to Vonny. She was startled at how different Vonny looked from the last time we had visited her together. Dementia was quickly taking Vonny's body and mind, making a notable difference with each passing day. Although she responded with nods when we spoke, it was clear that Vonny knew very little, if anything, of her surroundings. As Vonny sat in her wheelchair, my companion and I wrapped our arms around her and offered a companionship prayer. As usual, Vonny folded her arms and bowed her head. Unable to speak clearly, she hummed at the end, as if to say, "Amen." That month, the message was on eternal families. Shortly after that visit, Vonny joined her family in the eternities.

Vonny's funeral was lovely; her children and grandchildren told stories of her that she had not been able to tell me, which caused me to love her even more. In having the privilege of being the visiting teacher of such a precious soul, I learned something about visiting teaching that I did not previously understand. Visiting teaching is the act of charity; it is the pure love of Christ. In her state of dementia, Vonny taught me this. Our meetings were about sharing the spirit in a program that is inspired. Through her, I gained a testimony of Visiting teaching. Through her, I gained an understanding of the privilege it is to serve Christ. No matter how lonely or needy I was, I could still be of service.

The beauty of visiting teaching is not to see **100** percent on the monthly report; the beauty of visiting teaching is seeing lives changed, tears wiped away, testimonies growing, people loved, families strengthened, people cheered, the hungry fed, the sick visited, and those who are mourning comforted. Actually, visiting teaching is never "done" because we watch over and strengthen always. — Barbara Thompson, "And of Some Have Compassion, Making a Difference," General Relief Society Meeting, September 2010

AN ALARMING BEGINNING

I HAD A NEW companion—Naomi, a young mother with two toddlers and a famous husband in the sports world. Even though I was fast approaching grandmother years, I had a foster baby in tow, so we were a compatible pair. One sister on our list, Betty, was getting married. This would be Betty's fourth husband, and we hoped the last and best. Naomi and I wanted to do some special occasion interior decorating to surprise her. We made arrangements with Betty's son to gain entrance to her home during their absence. On a beautiful day, accompanied by the kids and baby, we went with streamers, hearts, candies, and shamrocks (the groom was Irish), and our wedding gift to do our best job.

We found the key and opened the door, only to be greeted by the screech of an alarm and a full-grown standard poodle, who quickly made his escape down the street. Mouths open, we contemplated our options. Since the dog had disappeared, we could not just turn and run without trying to find him. We also assumed the police would be coming soon. They did. They found us inside beginning to decorate with help from our wee crew. We told our improbable story, and they believed us! I suppose they figured no one could make up such a scenario. Furthermore, they were more than willing to help find the dog when Naomi offered a football autographed by her husband. The newlyweds were delighted with their surprise, the dog was returned home, and all continued happily ever after . . .

Actually, the marriage didn't last long, but my friendship with Naomi has continued, which was the real gift of that visiting teaching assignment. My daughter began babysitting for her children, my son has been home teacher to Naomi's family for years, and now my oldest granddaughter is a good friend to Naomi's daughter. Blessings journey through generations.

WHEN I WAS LITTLE

OUR UPSTAIRS LIVING room was full of the morning's smooth haze shining in through the big picture window. My mother and her visiting teachers sat there on the couch and chair in that room I was not allowed to play in, but I was four, and I stayed close. Their bodies stretched up and away from me, their heads small and dark. But their legs, at my level, were impressive—big, long legs in nylons, bent and tucked for proper sitting. I set up an obstacle course with the low, flat bench from the front entryway, a chair from the kitchen, and two couch pillows. I arranged them to approach the stairs and I became a snake, slithering below the bench, between the pillows, around the chair, and finally down the stairs, head first. From the bottom, I crawled up on two arms, pulling my long self behind.

Those women kept talking the whole time. I looked at them and began my slither again, listening for what they said. Surely they were talking about me. Of course they must have been. They noticed me. I felt it. I slithered more. Went down the cliff. It was hard work, and I did a good job.

I arrived back at the top again, and they were still talking. My mom was talking. The visiting teachers were talking. But it was not about me after all. I couldn't understand what it was they were saying. I found a sitting spot on the edge of the room and doodled my fingers in the air. They talked and talked. Stayed and stayed. They shifted their long, nyloned legs from side to side. My mother raised her voice as she did when expressing an important opinion. The visitors listened. There was more talking. Their voices became a soothing hum in that room and time and conversation where I still want to be.

MORE THAN A VISIT

MY MOTHER DIED five years ago at age seventy-nine. For several years her health had been failing. She was losing short-term memory and becoming physically frail. My two sisters and I lived states away and did what we could from a distance to buoy her, help her get assistance, and cajole her into taking care of herself. She was lonely and emotionally beleaguered by life's fast clip.

That last June, she came to visit our young family. It took some doing for me to switch gears from my frantic mother-of-busy-youngsters mode to walk at her pace and fill in her lapses. However flawed my efforts, we all noticed that with patience, kind words, and tolerant, tender care, she was beginning to flourish. By the end of her two-week stay, my little boy and I waved to her as she walked down the corridor to catch her plane back.

"I'm so grateful to you, sweetheart!" she called just before she got on the plane.

Three weeks later, she suffered a fatal stroke. I miss her so much. I can't believe it's been five years.

We moved to a new ward three years ago. One of the women I've been assigned to visit teach is Sister Scott, a spry octogenarian with thick, white hair. She is alert of mind and, though not robust, in good physical health. I love seeing her every month. I love being able in some small measure to practice patience, kind words and tolerant, tender care again for an elderly person. Sister Scott practices reciprocal gentleness with me. We're both flourishing in this relationship.

Sister Scott probably has no idea that she is helping me grieve and heal. When she opens that door and I walk into her home, I doubt she knows how timeless and wide her threshold is. I am so grateful.

LEGENDARY LIZA

VISITING LIZA IS the best calling I've ever had. She is a Londoner, through and through. She has stories ranging from the WWII Blitz (which has left her so traumatized that she sometimes spends whole days in her soundproof thunder shelter) to her hilarious experiences looking after "Dorothy" who lived in a box under Charing Cross Bridge.

Liza met Dorothy along the Thames River embankment. Dorothy rose like a phoenix from her cardboard box and asked Liza if she happened to have a cup of tea on her! From that beginning came a lasting friendship until Dorothy's death four years later. Liza and her beloved dog, Soul (who also used to come to church), traipsed miles across London every single day to take Dorothy lunch. Now that's visiting teaching! This was only ever missed during Liza's annual vacation, but the task was delegated to her home teacher who more than rose to the occasion by taking rather grand pâté sandwiches. "Spoiled her rotten," sniffed Liza.

Liza's hospitality is legendary. She must have fed more missionaries than the rest of the ward put together, turning out huge and mouthwatering feasts from a tiny kitchen, which she negotiates almost entirely by feel. She is legally blind and has recently had serious surgery to try to counteract a detached retina.

It is a great pleasure to keep her company and read the poetry she so loves—in particular Emily Dickinson, Ogden Nash, and some of the great Victorian poets. I was over there today with an anthology of Cornish poetry in my hand. In hers was a plate of smoked salmon sandwiches.

So many of us have been recipients of Liza's nourishment. This is not only because of what she offers to eat, but because she demonstrates true Christian behavior—the seeing of the soul inside, the loving of the unloved and the nonjudgmental meeting of a need.

MY UNCOMMON FRIEND

A T FIRST I wasn't sure if I liked being "assigned" to become friends with the women in my ward through visiting teaching. Shouldn't friendships develop naturally? Couldn't my visiting teaching assignments be to people I had something in common with?

That was before I was assigned to be Sister Trotter's visiting teacher.

Sister Trotter and I had very different backgrounds. I am a Yankee New Englander raised by upper-middle-class parents with access to many of society's educational and cultural benefits. I had three young children and a busy, employed husband. Sister Trotter was an elderly black woman, widowed many years. She was born in the Deep South long before integration. Her brother was lynched by a white mob. When we visited her, she lived with her unemployed son and three grandchildren in Philadelphia's toughest neighborhood.

Month after month, my companion and I visited Sister Trotter. In her quiet way she told us about her sorrows and joys. She spoke about the racial discrimination she and her family saw and suffered, the loss of her beloved husband, her mother's death on Christmas Eve.

We learned about her conversion to the gospel, her love of music, her appreciation for great literature, and her hopes and dreams for her grandchildren. She was genteel, intelligent, and gracious. She always greeted us warmly and hospitably.

Sister Trotter passed away a few years ago. I may have technically been her "teacher" during our years together, but Sister Trotter taught me more. By her example and her life—vastly different from mine—I learned about humility and grace, testimony and service, patience, forgiveness, faith, compassion, and courage. I am delighted to call her my friend and honored to call her my sister. I look forward to our next visit.

ACCEPTANCE

Washing my car is an every-other-month event because this is how often I drive for visiting teaching. I try to get out all the Cheerios, the graham cracker crumbs, the hair clips, the gum wrappers, the stray drinking straws, and the empty brown and wrinkled fast food bags. I taught with Anne for almost a year before I admitted this to her.

When I got Anne for my partner I was worried. She was sophisticated and had children who were almost my age. She was athletic, tall, lean, wealthy—lots of things that I was not. I had a dirt driveway; she lived in a home "up above." The contrasts embarrassed me.

I drove up to her house in my rumbling 1985 Volkswagen that had a rusting muffler we couldn't afford to fix. The horn didn't work either, but for once I didn't have to run to her door to get her because she heard me coming "for about five minutes before you got here." As she climbed in I apologized to her for my car and said to her—while waving my hand majestically over the dashboard—that I was hoping the cleaning job I had just done would distract her from the noise. I explained that she was the only person I ever cleaned the car for. She laughed and said, "Don't you know that I would go with you no matter what you drove?"

I had not known that our differences weren't important to Anne. She probably didn't realize how much her acceptance of our differences mattered to me.

PRACTICAL BITS

I'M THE KIND of person who works wells with lists. Here's a list that keeps me on track with my visiting teaching:

- Schedule appointments while still in the "single digits" of the month.

- Buy birthday cards for my sisters and clip them to the calendar for their birthday month, all stamped, addressed and ready to mail.

- Twice a year or so, take my sisters (individually or as a group if they know each other) out for some fun event (like for dessert or a dollar night movie or to watch a sunset somewhere . . .) Schedule this a couple months ahead of time to make sure our schedules work together.

- Keep at least mental notes on each sister's hobbies, favorite foods, and other personal information.

- Swallow hard and just make the phone calls.

The greatest service we can do in the visiting teaching business is to recognize each other as people, to know and care about each other's lives, to congratulate and empathize and try to comfort. We want to develop strategies that make it easy for people to visit us and easy for us to visit others. We want the time we spend together to be mutually enjoyable and enlightening. We want to accept each other as we are, as if we were, in fact, sisters.

TO MY VISITING TEACHERS
by Emma Lou Thayne

I'm glad you came, my friends.
Today was not a day marked on my calendar
in red—or black.
It was just a day.
Until you came.

You came to me
and I was all I had for you to see.
My props and backdrops, even my supporting actors
were somehow unimportant on the scene:

Just you. Just me. We three
in good companionship.

Or maybe, yes, I'm sure, there was another
who talked and laughed and felt with us.

Because, here now, behind the door
that I just closed
as you two touched my arm and said
you'd come again
the day is new
and I'm not alone at all.

Contributors

Alyson Beytien
Debra Blakely
Janet Brooks
Claudia L. Bushman
Harriet Petherick Bushman
Jeri Cardon
K Carpenter
Rebecca Walker Clarke
Emily Clyde Curtis
Sheryl Cragun Dame
Sheila Duran
Judy Dushku
Sherrie L.M. Gavin
Jeanne Decker Griffiths
Kristine Haglund
Suzanne Midori Hanna
Nancy Harward
Suzanne B. Hawes
Evelyn Bee Madsen Kimball
Linda Hoffman Kimball
Sarah Kimball Whisenant
Lael Littke
Marci McPhee
Lori Merkley
Steffani Raff
Carol Lynn Pearson
Amy Skouson
Kathryn Soper
Peggy Stack
Heather Sundahl
Ann Stone
Emma Lou Thayne
Mendy Waits
Ardith Walker

Blog posts adapted by permission
of the authors

"Why I Love Visiting Teaching" by Heather, Dec. 18, 2011, www. the-exponent.com

"November 2011 Visiting Teaching Message: Teacher's Choice- Conference Compilation" by Spunky, Nov. 3, 2011, www.the-exponent.com

"August 2011 Visiting Teaching Message: A Society of Holy Women" by Spunky, Aug. 4, 2011, www.the-exponent.com

"January 2012 Visiting Teaching Message: Watchcare and Ministering through Visiting Teaching," by Spunky, Jan. 5, 2012, www.the-exponent.com

"Census of My Sisters" by Guest, Nov. 6, 2011, www.segullah.org

"Never Faileth" by Kathryn Soper, Fall 2006, http://journal.segullah.org/category/editorial/

"Relief, Society" by Kristine, May 17, 2006, www.bycommonconsent.com

About the Author

A CONVERT TO THE Church, Linda Hoffman Kimball splits her time between Illinois and Utah. She loves dark chocolate, constructing collages, and creating forums where LDS women can share their stories and lives. She has compiled *Raspberries & Relevance: Enrichment in the Real World* and *Apple Pies & Promises: Motherhood in the Real World*, both of which follow the same collective format as *Chocolate Chips & Charity: Visiting Teaching in the Real World*. She is also the author of *Enriching Ideas from A to Z;* two humorous novels for LDS adults—*Home to Roost* and *The Marketing of Sister B;* and a children's picture book, *Come with Me on Halloween.* She blogs for Segullah.org and writes for the quarterly women's journal *Exponent II.*